Tools & Ornaments

SAINT JULIAN PRESS

POETRY

Praise for ~ Tools & Ornaments

In Tracy Rice Weber's *Tools & Ornaments*, shadows help us see who we are and fill in what might be missing, what we work to save. Mercy is found at the bottom of a purse, in the outline of a wrench, on the other side of a creaking screen door. The mother holds most secrets, and the tide gathers all in her wake, a weight, and compass for sons, daughters, and mothers to come. Somehow, here, memory is precarious but still precious. The minutia of our ordinary living adds up to an extraordinary love and harboring. These brilliant poems are odes to what we most overlook—the granular and gritty spun to silk in Rice Weber's deft hands.

—Remica Bingham-Risher
Soul Culture and *Starlight & Error*

Tracy Rice Weber's *Tools and Ornaments*, a multigenerational study of complex emotional territory, illustrates the poet's astonishing ability to embody images with imagination. These poems reveal bold devastation and radical tenderness, a monument to family devotion. She deepens our understanding of the human experience and renders us hopeful through divinity. Rice Weber's mastery of the Heroic Crown of Sonnets, skillfully interwoven through the book, presents an unprecedented accomplishment in contemporary poetry. Thirty years in the making, *Tools and Ornaments* teaches us to embrace vulnerability and live fully each day.

—Elaine Fletcher Chapman
Hunger for Salt and *Reservoir*

Each poem in this beautiful collection navigates the distance between the physical and emotional worlds. Rice Weber pays equal tribute to the tools and the natural phenomenae that shape and anchor our lives, so this book becomes a lifeline. Rice Weber is a keen and compassionate observer, and this collection is the best companion and antidote to loneliness or fear in a changing world.

—Marie Mutsuki Mockett
American Harvest: God, Country, and Farming in the Heartland

More than lyrics, a poem is both made and mystical, capable of holding the many languages of our joys and griefs. But it is no mere ornament — we keep the artifacts of our very living in the poem. In turn, the poem keeps us — allowing brief order and mercy, windows of truth lit by fireflies. If, as Tracy Rice Weber writes, *"a man may be/ remembered by what his hands made,"* the poet's craft is as exacting as any architect's or builder's. After the poem is made, it too must weather the vagaries of time and fickle readership. But I know these beautiful, exacting poems in Tracy Rice Weber's *Tools & Ornaments* will reward readers for a long time.

—Luisa A. Igloria
Maps for Migrants and Ghosts
20th Poet Laureate of Virginia, Emerita

Tools & Ornaments

Poems

by

Tracy Rice Weber

Saint Julian Press
Houston

Published by
SAINT JULIAN PRESS, Inc.
2053 Cortlandt, Suite 200
Houston, Texas 77008

www.saintjulianpress.com

Copyright © 2023
Two Thousand and Twenty-Three
©Tracy Rice Weber

ISBN-13: 978-1-955194-16-7
Library of Congress Control Number: 2023937314

Cover Art Credit: Christi Harris/ christilynnharris.com
Author Photo Credit: Allen M. Weber

FOR JACK & LINDA

CONTENTS

Traveling

The Level, the Coping Saw, the Claw Hammer	2
The Way You Still Blame the Dead for Unfinished Business	7
The Company I Keep	8
Leveled	9
july 1969	10
Because of a Michigan Farm Boy	11
Balancing Act	12
After Chemo	14
My Mother-in-Law in the Hospital, I Consider the Book of Ruth	15

Between the Green Tip & the Root

The Level, the Coping Saw, the Claw Hammer	18
You buy grocery store carnations to remind you	23
Objects in Mirror are Closer Than They Appear	24
Not a Lion	25
All that Keeps Me	32
Simple Comfort	33
First Aid for Seizures	34
Even Dead, my Mother is Unreasonably Difficult to Appease	35
Downsize	36

A Falling Weight, a Shifting

The Level, the Coping Saw, the Claw Hammer	40
For the Love of Plastic Acorn Capsules from Gumball Machines	45
Blink	46
Another Passage	47
Pawn	49
On a beach two hours after the school dance	50
Doves	51
Compostponement	52
Persephone Takes a Powder	53
Sometimes We Wonder Who We Used to Never Be Again	54
Etymology	55
Phone Call from First Born	56

We eat through tubes of time
as the cockroach,
as the apple and the codling moth,
as worms of neutrinos;
and what is not there
is always more than there.

                Ruth Stone
                from "Sorrow and No Sorrow"

Tools & Ornaments

Traveling

The Level, the Coping Saw, the Claw Hammer

My father found himself traveling—a buyer in retail, circling
home when he could to truer callings—handyman, dreamer
of impossible projects—a basement he tried to dig by hand
filling with rain, reason enough to spend weekends in the damp-

smelling garage. Maytag whirring, he traced tools
then painted their silhouettes—inventory on pegboard
where they hung. A practical matter, to see what was missing
by the shadows they left. Memorizing those shapes,

I learned the value of negative space. The work done bit

by bit there, the comfort—puzzling out repairs, favors
for neighbors, gifts for friends. What you might need—

a solid table, a sturdy mantel. He taught me how a man may be

remembered by what his hands made. He also taught me
sometimes what's missing serves mercy's greater cause.

*

Sometimes what's missing serves a greater cause:
mercy. Waxing and waning—the sound of driveway gravel
crackled against his wheels. In the background
of my childhood, the crayon-blue

mountains; in the foreground, a chain
link fence, the slender mimosa—its pink fireworks
and easy confetti, its crooked finger pointing
to another side where grass grew soft and thick

as shag carpet. I learned about safety there; how
to climb out. After supper some nights, he'd perform
jump rope cowboy tricks for neighbor kids, then pull us
around that field—hasty thrill, chain of children

running serpentine. Laughing, the blur of green
and blue, drunk with speed and chaos.

*

And blue, drunk with speed and chaos
he took on beastly features. Mother called them *spells*—
those blue-black nights he left and didn't come home.
I learned to protect her from his narrow eyes, his jaw pulled

taut; days later appearing in the shape of apology,
malleable like playdough after it spent time
unbothered in the can. Reborn that way, he could
build a treehouse between loblollies or a covered

wagon atop our Radio Flyer; he could pedal me
on the handlebars of my banana bike uphill
all the way to Howard Johnson's in the middle
of a Monday to choose from twenty-eight flavors.

He could be a hero whenever he could be. Then, work
clothes pressed, even his sweat smelled clean.

*

Work clothes pressed, his sweat smelled clean
on a Sunday when the Blue Law kept him mostly
home, oxford-cloth yard shirt tucked into his jeans,
work belt matching polished work shoes. Pressed

together, his lips stretched into a smile, he waved
at neighbors, *Hello!* I want to sit there on the cool
brick steps again, hugging my knees to watch him
broadcast, from an upturned fist, grass seed

to earth. Diligence, this work to make life appear green
on the outside—the front yard, pristine. When I
was six, he took a shotgun out of the closet and locked
himself in the bedroom. Mother knelt in the hall, her head

against the door, hand conjuring a lesser moon, *Jack, no.*
We depended on night's darkness to bear fireflies.

~ Tools & Ornaments ~

*

We depended on night's darkness to bear fireflies.
Maybe he'd just cut the grass—summer perfume. Maybe he
sat with Mother at the picnic table by the soft maple. Maybe
they shared a cigarette, spoke kindly when the heat gave up

pressing—the otherwhere of days. My father was proud of me
when I spit watermelon seeds the farthest. He was proud of me
for knowing tools by name, for reaching into my vinyl daisy purse
and asking, *Phillips or flat head?* I liked being near him then, watchful

bird over a project in motion. The even nature of his planting,
building, fixing. He used what he had to find brief order—
with the back of a flat shovel edged the walk, leveled rows of Arrowwood
along the cracked foundation of our house. Before he asked, I offered bypass

pruners for a nice, clean cut. There is where I try to keep him—tending
a garden's possibilities *between the green tip and the root.*

The Way You Still Blame the Dead for Unfinished Business

Maybe if you hadn't started at all,
if the canvas had just been left blank.
Maybe if there'd been no tubes of paint

to salvage from your old habit of unfinished
business, if the colors left had been in hues other
than grief. You sketched your parents, to later study

the light in a photograph your father took with a timer:
American Gothic in the early evening light. Mother
in her work heels, readers perched on her head;

Father in a loosened tie, two pens in his breast pocket,
on the steps of the house they'd suffered to build—
an image of success he hoped to document. Soon after

the final funeral, you found comfort loading
your brush to paint a background: the white tongue
and groove siding, a proud red cross and bible door,

dark windows, geometry you could count on as truth.
Years later, your mother and father wait for burnt umber
and raw sienna. They wait for the fleshing out of forgiveness.

The Company I Keep

I thought I'd outgrow a lullaby,
that long division worked itself out

eventually. With more years
than cakes could hold candles,

I wouldn't need your voice
calling hello, calling me awake

to question every station of the heart.
These pages are my mother now,

sorting out the broken bits,
dropping pennies in a jar.

Who can be more than you,
carrying me in your body?

I'll always see your lipsticked
mouth in the moon.

Leveled

        Once, you picked him   up at school for another

doctor's appointment
                you saw him   on the playground

his mainstream class   doing laps   to burn   off third-grade

enthusiasm   before the slog   back to cruelty   of seat work.

        That time   you saw him running

        among neurotypical peers   blonde hair   whipping

from his high brow   in late afternoon sun.

        That time   on the blacktop   he was more

beautiful   than all the others—   body lithe, unfettered   as wind.

july 1969

space was still   a magical buzz   day and night converged   with light   in 64
crayon colors raw umber   one plus built-in sharpener   with dish soap hands
she reached   for the glass milk jug   filled the tin measuring cup   placed it
cool against my hands   my looped pointer finger caught   the jagged edge
of the ear   it was coffee   i pretended   *what to drink   when you are grown up*

i was afraid   too high   funny to a young father   i clutched the chains
of the swing   too high *afraid*   maybe you'll kick   the moon he said   mother
whispered don't   wake your baby   brother in the pockets   of my culottes
wax lips and bazooka joe   wax bottles with colored sugar water   candles dripped
yellow wax onto the cake while   i tried   to make a wish that could   come true
i wanted a wish to come   true yellow pollen and white   ash from the paper mill
lawn chairs covered   in summer snow the clothesline   ran through the center
of our yard   two climbing maples   a mother and a father rusty   swing set sand
box in the corner   smelling of the neighbor's   cat chain link   fence squeak of

the gate   of the swing the screen   door smacking against   the frame porch
where the washing   machine churned bleached sheets   on sunny days hung to
dry a maze   of white tunnels led me   to her scratchy freckled legs   *read to me*
ogden nash from a child's   book of verse: *belinda   brave as a barrel of bears   ink
and blink and lions downstairs   mustard the tiger in a rage   custard the dragon in a safe cage*
and she took the clothes   pin from her mouth   pinched it   to the line   sat
down   cross-legged in clover   with a basketful of wet going   sour in the sun

Because of a Michigan Farm Boy

Golden apples in the garden:
while Atlas went for the prize
      Hercules held the weight of wanting—
      a wedding present to Zeus from Hera.

When he asked me to meet his family,
I'd never seen a Great Lake. In winter,
      Michigan orchards whispered white
      branches reaching for another season.

There were hardwoods
and quiet waterways
      he wanted to show me
      between Braeburn orchards.

He pointed to the trees
on Understory Farm,
      remembering what he'd stolen—
      a broken place in the fence.

Making pies with a grandmother
after school, September
      birthday candles
      breaking tender crust.

For a sapling to survive
you must wait for the last
      hard frost before planting.
      In Michigan, spring takes forever.

Eve wanted to sample all
things living. Why wouldn't she
      want to taste the sweet flesh?
      Why wouldn't she give in?

Balancing Act

Autism doesn't keep
        my eighteen-year-old son,
        my shopping wingman,

from understanding how
        these kinds of awkward
        episodes unfold. We retreat

from Checkout Line 4,
        abandon our cart of
        bagged groceries to find

a bunker in the privacy
        of the family van
        where I am grateful

for the miracle of
        Consumers Cellular
        and dial 1-800 numbers

on the back of every
        charge card I carry
        to find one

not currently maxed.
        Resigned, I pull
        from a glove box

emergency arsenal:
        a few crumpled bills.
        Back at the cash register,

I finger nickels and dimes
        toward the adjusted total
        and its minimized bounty.

The cheerful checkout clerk's
        crucifix earrings dangle
        to shoulders

not yet burdened
        with the weight of compromise.
        She feels compelled

to share the wisdom of her
        Sunday morning devotion:
        The Lord provides—

though today
        the Lord doesn't see the need
        to provide a box

of Chardonnay,
        a Boston Butt, or a bag of Cheetos.
        I consider the adventure

whenever I pull our cart up
        to a check out,
        my tank needling E.

I mean who needs sky-
        diving or rock-
        climbing or even

a summer pass
        to a theme park with such
        domestic thrills to be had?

God only knows.
        Counting on mercy again
        from the bottom of my purse,

we seal the deal
        when Checkout Girl
        hands over my

receipt with instructions
        to *be blessed* as if
        she'd lost faith

in *Have a nice day—*
        smiley faces stamped
        off center on two plastic bags.

After Chemo

Certain subjects I avoid—plans that reach
beyond arm's-length, for instance.

Her head—wrapped like a present, pink
bow above the ghost of her left brow.

We are here for sandwiches on fresh
bread, carrot juice, spinach smoothies—

organic. Our words step over sidewalk cracks
like the rhyme we said in school. Once,

we might have complained about gray
roots or sagging breasts, clueless

husbands, empty nests. Today
we exchange bird stories—how

one was trapped, despite the screen door
propped open. How she worked,

climbing on a rickety table, balancing
on a rocking chair, to pluck the wren

from the eaves of her porch, then
      release it into a heavy sky.

My Mother-in-Law in the Hospital, I Consider the Book of Ruth

You could say we didn't flock
together. Bird of a different feather,
she seemed to perch on a limb
for a better view of my reckless
indulgences: cut flowers, potted

annuals, multiple black sweaters.
She wore practicality
pinned to her breast like blue
ribbons from the county fair. Once,
she handed me a stack of Christmas

paper napkins to set the table
in July. To be fair, they matched
the tablecloth. *May as well use these up
than buy new...* And now I think
of Ruth who could have high-tailed it

back to Moab when she no longer had
solid reason to stay. I guess, loyalty
was her finest quality—compassion
before self-comfort. In quiet ways
of womanhood, I doubt I would've

passed such a test, though I wish
I could have suffered more for this
woman. How much easier to stand by
those who see us as we'd like to be
seen, who search for the same grace

from ordinary spaces, devoted to a reflection
from a glossy surface. In the Old Testament,
the Divine Author didn't see the need
to reveal whether Ruth was likeminded,
only that she was loyal for all her days.

Between the Green Tip & the Root

The Level, the Coping Saw, the Claw Hammer

Between the green tip and the root
Any point of a circle is its start:
Trying to find its way
        by a current I could not name or change.
In the framed black and white photograph
Divine shapes, scents, their sorrowful voices and silences.
Memory was the room I entered down a long corridor
        and the cold bleak lack to come.
What did I know, what did I know
Of your ice-hearted calling—
Of the Significance of This—
trying to get saved.
I was asleep while you were dying
        floating toward nightfall, out of otherwhere

The Level, the Coping Saw, the Claw Hammer (#6) is a cento comprised entirely of lines borrowed from the following poets (in order of appearance): Jane Hirshfield, Larry Levis, T S Eliot, Marie Howe, Ruth Stone, Michael Schmidt, Robert Adamson, Dorianne Laux, Robert Hayden, Sylvia Plath, Emily Dickinson, Tiana Clark, Natasha Tretheway, and Rosanna Warren.

*

Floating toward nightfall, out of otherwhere,
winter holds its place here. Foolish
daffodils push against a frozen ground,
work the odds they'll find spring
on the other side. By sunlight that's come

early across my kitchen's unswept floor,
another anniversary of his leaving
takes again his shirts and their salty smell,
the phone chats, the valentine mail. Takes his hands
that patted my hands. His fixing hands: the bike,

the car, the camera, the cut. But I must collect
myself each morning. Pack brown bag lunches
of sandwiches and apples for children. For them
I draw cloud shaped names, smiley faces.

~ Tools & Ornaments ~

*

A child, I draw cloud shapes and smiley faces
on construction paper. Each one I present, he pierces through
with a wire clothes hanger, unraveled like an arrow. There,
a stack of crayon art collects; the hanger's Barrel-of-Monkeys

arm looped on a closet door, practical filing for childhood love
letters: brick houses with triangle roofs, chimneys with curlicue
smoke; mother, father, children, and even the daisies smile.
You're tearing them, I say when I first see his method.

So I can keep them forever, he says. Thirty years later,
sorting souvenirs from broken colors, I recover
forever from a cardboard box. Lies work this way—
giving too much hope, impossible versions of stories.

In dreams my father travels from the purple moon
and back, to spare us all the wrong memories.

*

My father, to spare us all the wrong memories,
chose an escape hatch. There are worse things
than death, you come to learn. Shapeshifting is not like you see
on television: sudden flash, enchantment. It is, instead, a gradual

tearing of tender flesh. Slow torture, jagged gibbous. Wracked rupture
of a creature's fangs through human gums. We should've reckoned
he'd sort out Lycanthropy's terminal antidote, a gentler version
of the silver bullet, there in the comfort of his garage. I'm here

to tell you sometimes the monster suffers the unspeakable. Small boy
in a cramped house makes a fortress—closet door against carnal pillage
of brothers. There he crafts, with clever hands, airplanes from his own balsa
wood design. In that space, glue fumes let him believe he's flying.

But grown-ups must eke out a living; the boy puts away his useful
toys: the level, the coping saw, the claw hammer.

*

The level, the coping saw, the claw hammer—
What a man might need to build a frame for a rope
swing like the one at Uncle's farm, stretching up as tall
as a house. Every July, sweating in culottes, I ate only the crispy
skin of fried chicken, throwing the rest away before anyone noticed

I was wasting. Apple pies cut in quarters shared with removed cousins,
trolls from bridges, who'd be the ones to say *If it weren't for reunions,
we'd only see each other at funerals.* My father's laughter: the sound of copper
shaken in a jar. I wondered then if fireflies offered their dreams

to the light of day. I cried when he pushed me too high on that big swing,
knuckles white, gripping the coarse rope, my red PF Flyers
treading sky. He promised not to scare me, but he always did and
I never learned not to trust him, never learned *what doesn't kill you*

makes you—the storm approaching, his eyes turned from blue to gray.
The weight of the atmosphere shifted. A falling pressure.

You buy grocery store carnations to remind you

details are important when your work is
to usher the dying. You consider light and
its architecture a means of ascension. You

consider sound a vehicle for passage—
the music of footsteps, of breath. You
consider senses in turn, imprints

of the physical world which tend to land you
in flowerbeds. After so many seasons, certain
petals and perfumes call back hospitals and

funerals, apologies too late for resolution.
But mother always showed up before you
knew you needed her—like your need for

the warmth of yellow against
February's colorless earth. Every year
it reminds you of the temporary nature

of all that's green. Still, the daffodil is
your favorite flower: stupidly hopeful,
pushing up through the hard earth.

Objects in Mirror are Closer than They Appear

The good part about taking him to his 6am shift to make donuts is the chance
to impart subtle splinters of career advice. Shifting with the sharp turn
from Main St. to Mercury Blvd, I take a chance at *mom-talk*, sharing how
I'd always wanted to be one of the shoemaker's elves, working a tabula rasa thing,
leaving small miracles for someone to notice, or not, if only the pay
was a little better than minimum wage. He sits in the passenger seat, maybe
hearing parts of my rambling, silent because it's 5:50 am and still so sleepy,
stymied with dread over the prospect of *Buy-A-Dozen-Get-A-Dozen* Donut Week.
Then because I've turned into the parking lot and I'm swinging wide around
the drive-thru already three cars queued, before his perfunctory thank you, I go
full-monty Hallmark on him: *If you find work you really love, the money will come*,
to which he closes the car door with less of a slam than usual, perhaps because
he's tired or perhaps because he accidentally let himself feel a little hope
which I consider while I make with relative ease a usually impossible left turn
out of the parking lot, a caffeination of guilt taking over, serving my son such
jelly-filled lies. Turning into the safety of our cul-de-sac, lines of geese
in my rearview mirror cross a full morning moon. Here, such clichés of living,
an arrow pointing to a bull's eye—custard-filled against a sky of every color;
how far away to be seen so clearly.

Not a Lion

1

The fifteen-month-old climbs the winding staircase
of their duplex to the small bedroom he shares with
his two-year-old brother. The father is close behind,
his hands ready to catch should Baby stumble. Brother
has climbed ahead and shouts from his big boy bed,
I win! The small window at the top of the stair filters
early afternoon light onto Baby's white-blond hair. They
have just come back from a check-up. The father will call
the mother at work to tell her everything went fine. Baby
is in the top percentile for height and weight. He is mostly
on target with milestones. Baby and Brother will sing
the alphabet song with their father. He will read them three
books. This is their ritual before naptime.

He said *mama* and
dada and then he didn't.
The seizures began.

2

The doctor meets them at the Children's Clinic
on a Saturday. He is the doctor on call. He wears
a patient smile and Bermuda shorts. He tells the mother
and father it's common for new parents to overthink
new behaviors. Baby is just unsteady on his feet, losing
his balance then catching himself. Maybe he is weak, still
getting over a cold. Is he up to date on shots? Yes, yes.
Brother sits on the examining room floor and reads aloud
Ten Apples Up on Top. *Bess you*, he says without looking
up from the book when Baby sneezes. The father nods
his head at the doctor. The mother gathers her brow. When they
carry the boys back out into the brightness of the parking
lot, she will say to the father, *There. Did you see that?
Like a tic. He did it again.*

At the hospital
a kindly neurologist
advises them to pray.

3

After a battery of tests rules out tumors and brain injury, the pediatric
neurologist warns the mother and father there may be language delay.
Delay gives way to loss. For months, few words. None spontaneous.
Baby mimics sounds that have rhythm. The mother and father sing
Disney songs to fit every here and now. They mount a language board
to the kitchen wall: words he once used, words they would bring back,
words they would teach him. Now Brother is three. Baby plays alongside,
not with. A friend of the family utters the word, *Autism*, as casual
as weather. The mother will research. A light will die in her. For days she
will not be able to swallow. While she crushes half a tablet into powder
with the back of a spoon, Baby pushes a step stool across the black and white
tiles of their kitchen floor to climb up and watch her at the counter. He loves
applesauce; she always puts the crushed tablet in applesauce. After he sees
her sprinkle the powder he will not eat it again.

A counselor comes
to answer questions. *In time*
he may say your names.

4

The mother calls a friend—who lives in a big house in a fancy neighborhood—
with connections. She tells her friend maybe Baby just has a mind of his
own. That he refuses to jump through hoops. Brother hears her on the phone;
he interrupts the conversation to remind her that Baby won't jump through
hoops because *He knows he's not a lion.* The mother's connection gets Baby
an appointment for screening from the city school system right away.
He is made eligible for a special education preschool program. Their friend says,
*Don't think of the label as a negative. It's a way to get services early so he may not need them
later.* On his first IEP, the diagnosis reads PDD NOS, which means *we don't know
what this child's problem is.* A month and a half before Baby turns three, an orange bus
picks him up on the narrow street in front of their duplex. The father straps
Brother into the car and follows the school bus through all its stops all the way
to school. He watches Baby as the attendant helps him climb off the bus. He
watches Baby as his teacher takes him by the hand and leads him into the school.
He will drive home chewing his lip. He will call the mother at work to tell her
he saw Baby get to school just fine. He will tell her Baby did not cry; but
the mother will hang up the phone and she will cry.

Goals become measured
in clinical terms. He knows
more than he can say.

5

Baby is now a Boy. When the parents go to his preschool for an end-of-year assembly, the Boy bends down to admire a classmate's baby sister in a carrier. Teacher says the Boy likes babies. That maybe the parents should have one more. Brother says, *Not another one!* He cries and cries when they tell him he'll soon have another baby brother. The Boy uses phrases from videos to communicate his wants and needs, his frustration and his sense of humor. The parents think this shows how smart the boy is to borrow language in such a way. The doctors call it echolalia. Every night, the mother tucks the brothers in. Brother says, *Good night, Mommy.* The Boy whispers, *Good night, Sweetie.* When she says, *I love you*, he mimics her intonation. He has never said *I love you* to her without prompting.

The mother wonders
will the New Baby learn words
before the Boy does?

6

It is before the world is on social media. The internet is young.
The Boy is now in kindergarten. He has been labeled. The mother
and father consider the buzz from other parents, from friends, from
newspapers and magazines and television. They hear about children
who are "cured" of autism. They buy books. They research special diets
and special supplements and special therapies. They take off work
and put the whole family in the car. They drive two hours to a pediatrician
in another city. From her, they buy expensive supplements to detox
the Boy's "leaky gut." They take him off dairy; they take him off gluten.
This, in a time when special diet foods are not available in mainstream stores.
Nothing is covered by insurance, but they have to try everything. *Everything.*

And then it happens.
Without prompting he hugs her,
I love you, Mommy.

7

The Boy is five. He still uses television and movie scripts to express
complex feelings. He is able to tell them what he wants. He is able
to greet them all by name. He learns to write his alphabet with a paintbrush.
He helps the parents with the Baby Brother. He plays with Older Brother.
He loves to sing. One day, he will surprise the mother, pressing his own
syntax into a sentence of beauty and awareness. She is boiling spaghetti
for supper. He stands at the stove and watches the steam rising
from the big pot. *The sky is cooking, Mommy*, he points. *The sky . . . is cooking*.

To be a poet
without words. He finds a way
to tender his song.

All that Keeps Me

I didn't expect to find
      grief standing on the steps,
the porch light burned out,
      no moon; my brother's breath
slanting past me in italics,
      his news holding onto
an empty glass. Where
      was the messenger going
he hadn't already been?
      I heard my voice: *Did he
kill her?* My parents
      had finally arrived
on the right street: a green lawn,
      country club invitations—
every box checked.

      I didn't expect to feel
drunk with relief. Days later
      I'd find myself back
in my old room: a playpen where
      baby boys slept, a husband
snoring under the lace
      canopy of my childhood.
When the house was still
      I tiptoed down into their dark
garage to sit where he made
      his last decision. What
distance left before
      I lay down blame? There
are fathers and mothers for every
      space left in me.

Simple Comfort

After the appointment I look up the word
because then I might find a loophole,

create an escape from misunderstanding; but
dictionaries won't lie

even when I'm desperate
for the good omens

God and Webster might provide.
How does *pervasive* stack blocks against time?

Isn't he alphabet-singing earlier than most,
just as his brother did? What

kind of grief can ease the headwind they say
language will bring? Small miracle:

metric feet have walked us this far.
Now we begin again. A rebirth

of sorts—the pieces scattered, a jigsaw
puzzle impossible to assemble.

Questions should come with answer keys.
Remind me again how lucky we are.

Say *developmental disorder* with a full, clear
throat. Mention the ticker tape parade

under which we all march, wondering in
vain whether we might be spared. It could be

worse. Assuming divine insight may take
x-rays of the fracture, conjure logical formulas before I

yaw toward a calculus of changed values, thinking
zero plus anything will be enough.

First Aid for Seizures

Stand at the kitchen sink.

Take inventory of your serpentine life, the hum of the refrigerator, the *kankatank* of the washing machine, cartoons blasting from a television, long-abandoned. Three boys, two cats, a dog, and their ongoing timpani.

But this sound—

A thump; you pause for a long quarter-second before you start upstairs two at a time calling, calling his name.

Step One: Ease your son to the floor.

Step Two: Turn your son gently onto his side. This will help him breathe.

This has happened before. This cannot be happening again.

Step Three: Clear the area around your son of anything hard or sharp. This can prevent your son from injury.

When he was eighteen months, the specialist at the special hospital told you about a special book that listed all the special information you needed to know about this kind of special condition, this special myoclonic form.

You always did hate that word and all the heavy permanence of it. It should mean something unique and lovely but special was not what you wanted for your child. Not your child. Smart not special. Beautiful and bright like the others.

Step Four: Put something soft and flat, like a folded jacket, under your son's head. Since you will want to be as close to him as possible, you will likely cradle his head in your arms while his limbs twitch and saliva gurgles up his throat.

You will cry and you will say his name over and over and you will also beg God to make it all stop. You will do anything if it could just stop.

Step Five: Time the seizure. Call 911 if the seizure lasts longer than 5 minutes.

This will be a guess, of course, because no one in the house is looking at his watch; they are all looking at your son. Waiting for it to stop. And it does, but only for a very few seconds before it will begin again.

Even Dead, My Mother is Unreasonably Difficult to Appease

Please understand, I've worked overtime
to reconcile survivor's guilty balance
against fate or God's plan or whatever

you want to call the way shadows
surprise you with their puppet shapes.
For years, I've kept watch for a sign
to justify holding on to boxes of china and

clouded silver serving pieces. Their stories,
exposed to this atmosphere, have blackened.
What appears on the surface is more than

anyone should bear. Let's take turns
at comfort, Mother, letting them go to
a well-lit, vacant space. Places set
from another daughter's tidy cupboard.

Downsize

Swollen now,
summer turns a chest
of drawers into caskets
that stick. A grave chore, this
robbing of souvenirs,
this season for excavating
artifacts from our living.
The weight in sorting:
throw away/give away/keep.
And I can't quite let go of three
umbilical cords wrapped
in cotton handkerchiefs
or notebook paper envelopes
that failed to preserve the baby
teeth we exchanged for nickels
and dimes. What are these tools we keep
in hearts of chests and drawers,
pulled loose from tongue
and groove; in frames gone
wobbly through flurry of use?
In the attic I find a stone,
a valentine; a lavender vine still
holds a scent of some meaning.
I mean, I must have kept
it all for something.

A Falling Weight, a Shifting

A Level, a Coping Saw, a Claw Hammer

The weight of the atmosphere shifting, a falling pressure;
the German wildwood dense with silver birch, Scots pine, beech—naked, a boy
was found clawing the Shaggy Ink Cap, growling for air in ferns and green moss.
There are stories some wolfmen were tortured to confess their pact with Old Scratch
while some claimed they'd been spirited away—shapeshifters with no memory
of crimes: the mauling and tearing of human flesh, the violent survival. But this
little wolf was spared, saved from himself. King George and his court named their pet
Peter, this boy without speech who crawled along on four strange limbs until,

attracted to shiny things, he snatched a pocket watch, and the novelty ran dry.
History tells us a kindly farmer was hired to care for the boy who lived past seventy,
a collar around his neck. Who cares for our wolven souls? The lucky ones, discovered
on doorsteps. The others, left to soothe themselves, grow wilder, pull at their hair,
howl at a curious void; *boys being boys*. How could my grandmother have known
her little wolf would learn to hide his wounds, trying to take it like a man?

*

Some wolves learn to hide their wounds
control a way to take it   like a man

until a gun's hammer is cocked
sending mother brother and me

to hide behind locked doors
where we wait out the howls

a lone wolf must cry
to purge the fiery cycle

the gravity of another pitch
a swerve off the shoulder of the road

churning up that history in dust
he must have tabulated the loss

what was bought and sold
traveling on fumes   in a parked car

*

Traveling on fumes in a parked car
he dreams of flying to the purple moon and back.

When I was eight years old, my father called me
from my bed, despite Mother's objection, to sit before

our black and white set to watch, on a fuzzy screen, Neil
Armstrong take his lunar walk. *You'll always remember*

this miracle, he said, *how a man can be here and also so far
away.* Then, from the kitchen, he brought tin foil to fashion

a better reception, to work magic on television rabbit ears.
Years later, he wrote with the Cross pen every salesman

carries in his breast pocket: *Now I lay me down to sleep.
But this is taking longer than I expected. Need more hose.*

Drafting notes on a tissue box found in the glove compartment,
his fixing hands—they did what they could.

*

His fixing hands did what they could
in every house we lived because my father knew how to lay

a basketweave for brick walks, how to cut from a simple jig
a fortress of white pickets. Crafting illusions of safety: the heavy

drop-click of a deadbolt lock. Now as the sun drops its anchor, I find
my way back to his leaving. Again, I float in two spaces. Now, my own hands

are mother hands, winter-chapped, nail-bitten. Tools, not ornaments.
On Longstreet, firmly fastened to that otherwhere, buds on Bradford pear

trees risk the repercussion of release. In dreams he visits briefly,
Oxford shirt and silk tie, none the worse for journey. His Cross

pen clipped to his breast pocket. His shoes, new-penny shined.
How is it you find your way home? I ask. *Oh, daughter*, he smiles, *I can*

travel to the purple moon and back. I always liked to fly.
Jack of all trades, my father, traveling still.

~ Tools & Ornaments ~

*

My father found himself traveling—a buyer in retail, circling
home when he could. We came to learn what's missing serves
a greater cause. He might be drunk with speed and chaos
but his clothes were pressed; his sweat smelled clean.
Depending on the night, his darkness might bear fireflies,
a garden's possibilities between the green tip and the root.
Floating toward nightfall out of otherwhere,
I still find him in cloud shapes and smiley faces.
My father, to spare us all—found ways to fix what was
broken. A level, a coping saw, a claw hammer—might mend
the weight of an atmosphere shifting, a falling pressure.
He learned to hide his wounds, to take it like a man.
      Traveling, parked car running in his garage, hose and exhaust pipe—
      his fixing hands—they did what they could.

For the Love of Plastic Acorn Capsules from Gumball Machines

In this one you found empty space
        salty erasers for every pencil in your case
        a formation of birds pointing you home
        smiling starfish and an entire ocean
        a lilac bush in bloom
        and the dream of flying

In this one a cloudy sky
        a runaway balloon on a road less traveled
        your mother's love
        bandage for a bleeding wound
        just a sliver of the great big moon

At what point did you want only the coin to fit the slot
        at what point lost the want
        of wanting?

When was there no more
        awe no more magic in what might
        roll down the silver chute
        to your cupped hands waiting?

Blink

Our Weekly Reader explained, they use oxygen with luciferin
    to produce light without heat. Somebody's going to die,
grandmothers warned, if one flies into the house. I knew it
    took a good twelve or more to light up an empty jar.

At dusk after school let out for summer, we ran barefoot on clay
    banks of a creek to catch them, a competition for luminary points. Before
neighbor boys mixed in, simple communion was enough. We stood under pines
    waiting to charm one from the night, to watch it land on an outstretched

hand, crawl across our palms and down our fingers, open
    wings and lift off, returning to the dance.
Miss Mead told class their blinks attracted mates. Even then
    I considered the hazard of making sparks, oblivious

reaction, without heat and without trying.
    It was Down-the-Street Boy who gave me my first ring.
Catching my elbow, he plucked the firefly from my finger,
    pinched its black head and, privileged

as a surgeon, separated luminous jelly from abdomen,
    rubbing his sticky crime against my knuckle.
Along the creek, girls with glowing fingers played tag on damp clover.
    By September, we barely noticed they were gone.

Another Passage

I brought for her bedside
a small lamp from home,
white ginger jar.
For some reason, I thought
she might need the low light.
I could give her little else

than robin egg blue
butterflies, light-
winging spirits.
In darkest morning
she might be cold,
but I was the one

who needed to be
tucked in, smoothed.
Through hospital mini-blinds
I thought I saw a circling
of crows—a sign for death
she once told me.

As children we kept a bird
with a yellow top hat
on the windowsill;
its round red beak
dip-dipped into a juice
glass to tell us what

we could already see
for ourselves: heavy
clouds yield rain.
We waited for the doctor's
rounds. There'd be no surprise
conclusions. The clouds

low, expectant. What else
can be made from the labor
of passage? It was this way:
She's gone
said the nurse.
Thank you, I said,
allowed
to worship her then,
her pale freckled skin

and parted lips.
She was still
there in the room
but we didn't care
to speak. Tell me
what isn't death when

life sets its intentions
toward that end? Who'd blame
anyone for counting on
fingers, the math of mortality?
Obstacles set against the need for
comfort played by ear

on black and white keys
a handful of tunes—
Heart and Soul,
Flight of the Bumblebee,
but only the first few
measures. Never the whole song.

Pawn

You've made this list before. Still, you're compelled
to write it: milk, bread, bracelets. You slide gold
bangles from your wrist; place them on the counter—
a scene recalling the O. Henry story you read in school.

You ask, *How much are they worth?* The young man shifts
in his Doc Martens. You wonder if his nose ring was purchased
in-house, originally a set of two from somebody's
once-upon-a-jewelry-box maybe bartered by a thief.

Maybe everything is bartered in the end. You wished
you'd gone to another neighborhood, another town. Not here
beside your favorite Food Lion. A plump woman, heavy foundation
and penciled brows, sits at a metal desk behind him. Perhaps

she is his mother. This transaction might feel less dubious if it were
a family business. *These are family pieces*, you hear yourself say
and bite your lip, trying to ignore reflection in the mirrored wall.

He tests heirlooms with a magnet, disinterested. Turns them over
to the woman at the desk. She's making a list with the nub of a pencil.
Without looking up, she offers your grandmother's engraved initials

to the scale. Muzak is the soundtrack of betrayal. The sun beats through
the shop window. You drag a sleeve across your face, ask *Is it hot in here?*
Gets hot around this time the woman says. With cash to buy a week's groceries,
you finger the bills in your pocket like a love letter you're anxious to read again.

On a beach two hours after the school dance

you didn't know his middle name (Edwin)
or favorite color (yellow like a blinking caution
light you might drive under, kissing your thumb
to the roof for luck.) His Chevy Impala with whip-
lash antenna. Zeppelin blaring, windows rolled
down, he drove faster than he should've. Wind
tangled your hair across your face so it was hard

to see where you were going. In eleventh grade
he was your date and you held your ground;
then, you were still just a new girl. You thought
love worked this way, in a tent late at night—a secret.
Sand stinging your face and legs, you remember
how it found you when he opened the flap;
the outer banks colder than you'd expected.

Doves

It might've been because we wanted boys
to think of us as fighters, not lip-glossed sweethearts
in monogrammed sweaters and add-a-beads—

those sorority girls who viewed us with contempt,
the hoi polloi in flannel shirts. In that season
to hunt birds, we joined co-ed killers.

Crouching among late September weeds,
we'd avoid our turn to take a shot against
the gray geometry, an augury at dusk. What

could they feed besides an ego? At the party,
olive branch decoys: single bites of consolation
lined on a grill. My college roommate lit

two smokes and passed one to me.
And frat boys rehearsed lies, sucking
their fingers as live coals died.

Compostponement

I didn't ask for it, but there I was without choice, taking on
the narrow-cushioned discomfort of my mother's camelback sofa.
When its feathers were fluffy and my hips not so much,
long before the upholstered arms claimed turf in my living
room, it was prime real estate for popcorn & TV, afternoon naps;
but charm fades when we find ourselves dragging the bulk

of history through our own front door. What compels a woman
to enlist as time*keeper*—mater of all family matter, sovereign of stuff?
Every room and closet cram-packed, I practice the art of the passive
aggressive purge. If picnics are packed with fine china, for instance, a set
eventually breaks down. Not even dead grandmothers would begrudge
hauling away plates with chips, saucers without cups. Any *thing* becomes,

at last, too broken for salvation; but that strategy's a mighty slow leak.
A therapist once told me I was *magical thinking,* which I took as a compliment
until boxes lined the walls. *Wood and cloth and glass do not have feelings, are not
attached to the spirits of the people we love.* But what about the rocking chair—
the back cushion, still fanned with her hairs—*living* there—though the rest
of her body knows minimalism by nature, the only way to go.

Persephone Takes a Powder

She pulls her Pinto up the drive before sunrise
to find their kitchen door unlocked. A coffee pot spits

and sighs. She imagines parents moving
through the morning's liturgy—

her father's whistling shower, her mother's electric curlers,
the light cast from another cycle of TV news.

The prodigal daughter waits at the breakfast table,
fidgeting with her car keys. Only a year and a half ago,

before giving her away, Father chalked falter up to cold feet;
but Mother raised waxed eyebrows: *Let's consider what's done*

can, indeed, be undone. Hands may be washed, losses cut. So much
in this life is at least partially refundable. If only Hades was a broker

in familiar ways, Persephone might have guessed how heat
first makes the radiator whine and moan. Eighteen months later,

she crawled into her childhood bed as if to ride out
the flu. Mother never said *I told you so*, only whispered

there, there tending Persephone's wounds
with sips of bourbon from a silver spoon.

Sometimes We Wonder Who We Used to Never Be Again

Our one and two-year-old sons
down for an afternoon nap,
we once took advantage of the couch to
sleep because it's not like you think—

parenthood. At least, not for the us
of our former we, slipping loose like
ribbon, its perfect bow around a gift
wrapped with onion skin paper—fragile and

translucent the way epidermis can't help but reveal,
from an ultra-sound, how we'd lost ourselves
to the cause. And nobody would be surprised
we cried at the first sight of each image,

alien beans from the inner space of origins. We
didn't know, did we? How quickly the vertigo
of pheromones steadied us to another pace, as if
      to walk with certainty into a bog, deep and heavy,
      necessary and true as soil and rain.

Etymology

After twenty-six years, he still flirts with me—
sharing honeyed Words of the Day.
He sends only those choice syllables
he is certain I'll want to possess.

Sharing honeyed words of the day
like *halidom, a holy place*
he is certain I'll want to possess,
to hold in my mouth like a deep kiss.

Like a halidom, this holy place,
he sends only those choice syllables
to hold in my mouth like a deep kiss.
After twenty-six years, he still flirts with me.

Phone Call from First Born

We lassoed you
                      from the night sky.

From dreams you cried us
to life.

            I pressed your hand

to my mouth: never close
enough.

                      Years erode

a shoreline—the rhythm of waves,
like breathing. I can't

siphon you back from the ocean.

The boatswain-bird   isn't   so much lost
as tired.   Perhaps this time

he flew   too far
                          from home.

ACKNOWLEDGMENTS

Sincere thanks to the journals in which earlier forms of these poems first appeared:

Barely South Review: "Simple Comfort"
Bangalore Review: "Not a Lion"
River River: "After Chemo"

All That Keeps Me, a chapbook published by *Finishing Line Press*, 2021.

Heartfelt gratitude to my dear family, good friends, attentive mentors, poetry cohorts, and devoted instructors who have supported and encouraged the creation of this book.

ABOUT THE AUTHOR

Longtime educator Tracy Rice Weber now teaches undergraduates at Old Dominion University and poetry workshops for The Muse Writing Center in Norfolk, VA. A graduate of the ODU MFA Program, her work can be found in *River River*, *The Bangalore Review*, on Poets.org as a recipient of the Academy of American Poets College Poetry Prize, and forthcoming in CALYX. In 2021 her chapbook, *All That Keeps Me*, was published by Finishing Line Press. She lives with her husband and two of their three sons in Hampton, VA.

Typefaces Used

TYPEFACE GARMOND - Garamond
TYPEFACE PERPETUA TITLTING MT – LIGHT

www.ingramcontent.com/pod-product-compliance
Lightning Source LLC
Chambersburg PA
CBHW080605170426
43196CB00017B/2909